Contents

Introduction

A polygraph examiner will say "You only need to tell the truth and you'll pass". He may also tell you "As long as your honest, you have nothing to worry about". Both statements are true, most of the time. Let me repeat that last part, most of the time. If you are abnormally nervous, if your mind is racing on various thoughts, or if you simply question your own memory, you may have a problem with the polygraph test. This problem can exist, even if you telling the truth.

This book will take you by the hand, and guide you through the polygraph examination process. It will destroy the intimidation factor by dissecting the polygraph from both a physiological and psychological standpoint, minus the unnecessary technical jargon. After reading this book, you will have the confidence, knowledge, and metal capacity to pass any polygraph exam, at any time.

If you are reading this book, then you obviously have concerns with taking a polygraph exam. Put your mind at ease. This book is a short, easy read. It will get straight into the information you need to be successful. It will not overload you with any information that will cause undue stress.

. Chapter 1

Blind Faith in the Polygraph

Technologically speaking, the polygraph is somewhat complex device. It consists of both mechanical and electronic components, that ultimately translate feedback from your body to the polygraph examiner via computer software. The polygraph examiner, then interprets this information and forms his or her professional opinion based on their training and prior experience.

Throughout my career, I have met several polygraph examiners and successfully undergone 7 polygraph tests. Most examiners were retired police officers that took up a second career. One of the examiners was a college professor of mine. Of all the examiners, this college professor was the most forthcoming with information regarding the validity of a polygraph examination. He was a full time polygraph examiner and part time professor. He had an impressive list of credentials, including polygraph experience in the federal field. He had a large amount of faith in the polygraph machine, but he stated that someone with a "very strong mind" could defeat the polygraph test, even while being completely deceitful. One day during class

went off on a tangent and lectured at length about the relationship between body and mind. The

gist of the lecture was, the body will follow the mind, but only if the mind is exceptionally strong

and well disciplined. The class was not on anatomy, physiology, and certainly not about

polygraphs. But this professor enjoyed speaking about his day job every chance he got. On the

last day of the semester, he brought a polygraph machine to class. He challenged anyone to try

and defeat the test by lying. A few students tried and failed. I wanted to to challenge the

professor's test, but I wanted to get out of class even more. Shortly after college, I gained plenty

of experience with taking polygraph examinations in the law enforcement field.

As for the other polygraph examiners, Although they were my brothers in law

enforcement and respectable individuals that I hold in high regard, I found them to be

overconfident in the polygraph test. They spoke of the polygraph as if it was the only true way to

decipher fact from fiction. I don't know if they really thought if was infallible or they only spoke

of the polygraph in that manner to justify their jobs.

Make no mistake, the polygraph can, does, and will uncover deception in most. Thats

because most people don't understand how to control their body's normal responses while

undergoing a polygraph examination.

Chapter 2

The Questionnaire

When you arrive at the polygraph location, where ever it may be, it seems to always be cold. This may intensify your anxiety or make you even more nervous. Don't worry about that. You will learn to ace the polygraph regardless of how nervous you may feel. We'll touch on this more in the Baseline chapter.

You will most likely be given a questionnaire to fill out. It will have the traditional identifying information questions as well as some general questions about you past employment. It may also have some of the actual polygraph questions such as:

Do you intend to tell the truth during the examination?

Have you ever stole from an employer?

Have you ever done illegal drugs?

and so on and so forth.

Do not begin to read deeply into the questions or second guess your own integrity. An example of second guessing yourself is asking "Does it count if I took a pen home from work". I doubt there is any employer that cares if you took a pen or pencil home. Furthermore, it's ridiculous to label yourself a liar or thief over a pen, pencil, notepad, or other such nonsense. The point I'm getting at is, don't psych yourself out before the test has even started. As a matter of fact, don't psych yourself out at any point of the process. Just answer your questionnaire and make sure to give the same answers that you gave on your original employment application and or background history statement. If you change any of your answers during the polygraph stage of your hiring process, this will be ammunition for the polygraph examiner to dig deeper and possibly label you as someone with questionable integrity. Yes, the examiner will cross reference the answers you give him with the answers you gave on your employment application.

Complete the questionnaire and continue focusing on the confidence and conviction you have about all of your answers. We will go deeper into exactly how to establish your confidence and conviction in later chapters.

Chapter 3

Meeting the Examiner

The examiner will come out to greet you. Smile, be personable, and feel confident. Not cocky, but confident. Know the difference. He will lead you to the exam room which is usually a typical looking office room. I once met an examiner at the University of California, San Francisco. He actually had a mobile setup in a hallway that wasn't being used. Yes, he still somehow managed to pick the coldest area in the entire school. That time, I was shivering from being so cold. Having said that, now you know you can actually be shivering and still pass the test. I'll tell you more about how and why this is possible in the Baseline chapter.

Your examiner will ask you if you have ever had a polygraph test before and make some sort of small talk. He will explain what equipment he is going to put on you. He will also tell you the questions he is going to ask you and explain that he will be asking you the same questions three different times. This means he will ask you a set of 5 or so questions, stop the test, then repeat the questions. So it feels like you are taking the same test, three different times.

The reason he will be repeating the test three times is to analyze your body's responses for any inconsistency between the questions. Notice I said "your body's responses" and not your mind's responses. The polygraph machine, nor the polygraph examiner can read your mind. He will also check if you answered all three sets of questions the exact same way. Do not change your answers for any reason. He doesn't even need the polygraph to suspect deception if you give inconsistent answers. We'll get into the actual question answering in later chapters. The purpose of this chapter is to give you an idea of what the examiner is going to talk to you about when you meet him.

Most polygraph examiners have great communications skills and will be courteous. But, don't worry about their demeanor. Your only concern is complete mental focus on certain bodily responses to stress. Further in this book, I will address these bodily responses in detail.

Chapter 4

The Equipment

After you sit down, the polygraph examiner will fit you with a blood pressure cuff, two galvanometers, and a pneumograph.

The blood pressure cuff is self explanatory.

The galvanometers are finger plates placed on two of your fingers. These small devices measure the amount of sweat you are producing as a result of stress.

The pneumograph is a set of tubes placed over your chest to measure the amount of air you are breathing into your lungs. It basically expands and retracts to measure the rate and amount in which you are breathing.

These three devices, will be recording three bodily responses that you will control. The three bodily responses are:

1. Your blood pressure

2. The sweat in your fingertips

3. Your breathing

All three functions are controllable by you. They are only autonomic bodily responses to stress, when you are not aware that they are occurring. In the case of a polygraph test, you are completely aware and you will be completely in control, regardless of your stress level. This is how;

Remember, you will need to answer the examiner's questions the exact way you answered them on your employment application, your personal history statement, and or your pre-polygraph examination questionnaire. If you answered, "I have never smoked marijuana". In your mind, you need to know for a fact and without a doubt that you have never smoked marijuana. If you need to trick yourself into believing you never smoked marijuana, think of a time in your life when you know for certain, you did not use marijuana. For example, when you hear the question "Did you ever smoke marijuana?", in your mind, think "When I was in middle school, I did not smoke marijuana". You can apply this mental scenario of being in middle school to help your bodily responses stay consistent throughout the entire polygraph session. Reason being, your recollection of middle school was in a time of innocence. It was a time before outside influences changed your values or decisions. Simply put, you knew nothing of marijuana when you were still in middle school.

The above mental lesson applies to those who were actually still good kids in middle school. Some kids were smoking at 12 years old. Use common sense and choose an innocent time of your life to recall when undergoing stressful questions. This will be especially useful to bypass employment disqualifications, such as past drug use or other such misdemeanor offenses.

The polygraph examiner will undoubtably ask if you want to change any of your answers before the test begins. He will offer you a chance to "come clean" by saying phrases like "Now is the time you can change your answers" or "Is there something you would like to add to your questionnaire". Don't fall for this trick. Stick to your original application answers and do not falter.

I will go further into detail of the individual components of the polygraph in separate chapters. Each piece of equipment placed on your body requires a different skill to master.

Chapter 5

The Baseline

After you are fitted with the blood pressure cuff, galvanometers, and pneumograph, The examiner will need to establish a baseline. This is to measure how nervous you are now. If you are cold or shivering, he will establish that during the baseline and account for it. This is necessary to avoid a false reading once the actual test has begun. The baseline also serves the examiner by giving him an idea of how your body will respond when you are being truthful versus deceptive.

Before the examiner starts the polygraph machine to read your baseline, calm yourself. Remember that you are only here to answer truthfully about a specific time in your life, that you choose to recollect. Regardless of what you are asked, in your mind, any and all questions are pertaining to that specific period of time. A time when you were in elementary school, middle school, in the military, or whatever time you choose to focus on.

The examiner will ask you identifying information that he already knows is factual and true such as you name and date of birth. He might also ask you if you are in an office with gray carpet, if you are actually in an office matching that description. The purpose of this is to read your baseline while your are in fact being 100% truthful. Then he will ask you to deliberately lie. This can be done a number of ways. If the carpet is gray, he may ask you to say the carpet is blue when he asks again, "What color is the carpet in this office". The idea is, when you lie, he should be able to see your physiological changes on the polygraph when compared to your readings as you are telling the truth. In other words, he will notice a break in consistency when you switch from honest answers to deceptive answers.

In addition to controlling your body's responses during questioning, you will also stack the baseline test in you favor. As I mentioned earlier, calm yourself. By this time, you will probably be as calm as you are going to get in this room. You will realize your own level of anxiety and have an idea of the level of focus you are going to need to control your blood pressure, breathing rate, and perspiration output at your fingertips. Answer your baseline questions exactly how you are going to answer the remainder of the questions during the process, with the exception of the lies the examiner will instruct you to give.

When he asks you to lie about the carpet color or a number you are thinking of, this is when you will intentionally loose your focus. Let your breathing rate change before you answer, let the feeling of anxiety surge to your fingertips. This intentional loss of concentration will automatically change your blood pressure. This will tell the examiner that you are being deceptive when your body reacts in this manner. However, after the baseline portion is over, you will need to maintain your focus and consistency for the remainder of the polygraph exam.

Notice throughout this book, the words "focus" and "consistency" are used on almost every page. These two words are paramount to successfully passing a polygraph examination.

Chapter 6

The Galvanometers

You probably never thought about it before, but when you get nervous, you might feel a slight tingling sensation in your fingertips or toes. This is especially noticeable in people afraid of heights, when they are near the edge of a building or other similar situation. This is where galvanometers come into play. Galvanometers are small plates placed on two of your fingertips. They will measure the sweat, obviously produced from your finger tips. An abnormal amount of stress will cause your body to produce more sweat. Your body will naturally produce a consistent amount of moisture at your fingertips. The key word here is "consistent". Natural and consistent is good. What you don't want is to produce more perspiration when answering a question.

During the polygraph exam, prop your fingertips on the edge of the desk in front you. If there is not a desk top, prop your fingers at the edge of your knee so that only the tips of your fingers and galvanometers are hanging off the edge. It's almost like you are trying to limit the amount of circulation going to your fingertips by using the edge of the desk or your knee. In actuality, this will not be effecting your blood circulation at all. It will however, help to

concentrate your focus on not letting your nervousness or anxiety transfer to your fingertips. If a

surge of anxiety comes over you, thats fine. As long as you do not let it effect, your blood

pressure, your breathing rate, or those two fingertips. This imaginary blood pressure restriction

method, in your mind, will prevent any surges of anxiety from effecting your fingertips. Do not

fidget around or move those two fingertips during testing. Think of those two fingertips as

completely non-functional, but by your own will. You are in control of your body, not the

polygraph equipment.

The only time it is okay to slightly fidget or move those two fingertips is during the

baseline phase, when asked to purposely lie.

Chapter 7

The Blood Pressure Cuff

The examiner will strap a blood pressure cuff to one of your arms. It is just like the one you are familiar with when you visit the doctor. When the test starts, it will fill up with air and become tight on your arm. When the test stops, the examiner will release the pressure. The blood pressure cuff measures the sound your blood makes as it pulses through your arm. The more nervous you get, the more BPM or beats per minute the blood pressure cuff will relay to the polygraph machine. Don't get caught up in the BPM thing. BPM is just an example to covey that the blood pressure cuff measures the amount of blood pulses your body makes in a certain amount of time. You only need to know how to keep you blood pressure consistent throughout the entire test. Blood pressure is mostly effected by your breathing, which is completely controllable by you.

Although you don't want to let your anxiety level get out of control, what you absolutely must focus on is the consistency of your blood pressure rate. Some might argue that blood pressure is a completely autonomic response to stress. I have first hand experience, on multiple

occasions, and beg to differ. You absolutely can control your blood pressure for limited amount

of time, especially in a controlled environment like an office. Other than the examiner's

questions, there are no outside stress factors or surprises that may influence your blood pressure

or stress level. At this point, any stress you have, is all in your own head. It's okay to have stress,

but you need to focus on maintaining a steady clam train of thought. Don't loose your focus.

Don't let your mind wander too far from your present situation, or else the next question may

surprise you. Breath normally, speak calmly when answering the questions, and do not squirm

around in the chair. Although the chairs are never comfortable, concentrate on relaxing your

body. Think to yourself, "I am telling nothing but the truth". "The truth is all I know". Do not

just tell yourself this phrase. Believe it. Believe it throughout your mind, in your bones, and in

your heart. Do not think of any of your past discrepancies in life. No one is perfect. Do not let

any of your dark moments haunt you.

In regards to your blood pressure, remember, to breath normally and consistently. If you

are too nervous to breath normally, you will need to intentionally take slow and easy breaths

throughout the exam (except when instructed to lie during the baseline).

Chapter 8

The Pneumograph

The pneumograph is used to read how much and how ofter you are breathing air into your lungs. Two rubber tubes will be placed around your chest. As your thoracic cavity expands and contracts, the pneumograph relays information to the polygraph.

Of the three bodily functions discussed in this book, your breathing is by far the easiest to control. Take normal breaths. Answer your questions, which are normally "yes" or "no", just before a normal exhalation. Do this so that you answer yes or no at the beginning of the exhalation and continue the exhalation after the word leaves your mouth. Answer just as you normally would in any conversation. Under normal, non-test situations, people usually answer a question just before they exhale. They don't normally take a breath and then answer a question unless there is some sort of stress factor involved. So, you should not either.

Your breathing will effect your blood pressure rate as well as your perspiration rate.

Maintain consistent breaths and the other two functions will follow. Remember the thoughts of your pre-selected time of innocence. The time that you have no reservations with speaking about. The time that causes you no stress whatsoever when answering questions about it.

Answer all questions during the polygraph in the manner described above, except when you are asked to purposely lie during the baseline phase. This would be the time to take a breath first, then answer with the intentional lie the examiner instructed you to give.

Chapter 9

Summary

In summary, the most important thing you must take away from this book is that if your mind believes you are being truthful, your body will respond accordingly. Control your thoughts and interpret questions the way you want to interpret them. Interpret questions as if they are only applicable to time period of your choosing. A time that causes you no stress when recollecting any subject matter. In other words, hear what you want to hear and think what you want to think.

Consistency and focus are both key to success. Be constantly aware of the three bodily responses and three pieces of equipment discussed in this book. If you do this, you will never have a problem passing a polygraph examination.

There are reasons why I did not include more technical information about the polygraph system. Disregard any information may have previously read on the internet. I've read most, if not all of it. The internet articles will only disrupt your focus by adding unnecessary thoughts and information to your mind when undergoing polygraph questioning. Simplicity is why you will be able to master your thoughts and bodily responses. It does not take a particular person with unusually strong mental strength or discipline to pass a polygraph. There are endless aspects to our anatomy and physiology, but you only need to focus on three of them. Breathing, blood pressure, and perspiration of only two fingertips.

This information will work for good people, who made a few minor mistakes in the past. The whole purpose of this book is to help you get hired with a potential employer and be a positive, productive, and generally good member of society. Not to put a detrimental person in a position of power or authority.

I would wish you good luck, but you don't need it. You now possess the knowledge and skill needed to successfully pass a polygraph exam.

www.ingramcontent.com/pod-product-compliance
Lightning Source LLC
Chambersburg PA
CBHW021002180526
45163CB00006B/2465